FUTURE **PERFECT**

JOHNS HOPKINS: POETRY AND FICTION
Wyatt Prunty, General Editor

FUTURE **PERFECT**

Poems by Charles Martin

JOHNS HOPKINS UNIVERSITY PRESS   Baltimore

This book has been brought to publication with the generous assistance of the John T. Irwin Poetry and Fiction Endowed Fund.

Johns Hopkins University Press
2715 North Charles Street
Baltimore, Maryland 21218-4363
www.press.jhu.edu

Library of Congress Cataloging-in-Publication Data
Names: Martin, Charles, 1942– author.
Title: Future perfect : poems / by Charles Martin.
Description: Baltimore : Johns Hopkins University Press, 2018.
Identifiers: LCCN 2017039402 | ISBN 9781421425351 (pbk. : acid-free
    paper) | ISBN 1421425351 (pbk. : acid-free paper) | ISBN
    9781421425368 (electronic) | ISBN 142142536X (electronic)
Classification: LCC PS3563.A72327 A6 2017 | DDC 811/.54—dc23
    LC record available at https://lccn.loc.gov/2017039402

A catalog record for this book is available from the British Library.

*Special discounts are available for bulk purchases of this book. For more
information, please contact Special Sales at 410-516-6936 or specialsales
@press.jhu.edu.*

Johns Hopkins University Press uses environmentally friendly book materials,
including recycled text paper that is composed of at least 30 percent post-
consumer waste, whenever possible.

For Wyatt and Barbara

CONTENTS

FUTURE **PERFECT**

DISCONTENTS

Owing to uncommon tastes and all too common poses,
There isn't any single scent pleasing to all noses:
This one, says Petronius, plucks thorns, and that one,
   roses.

ONE

WHEN WE HAD IT ALL

Our automobiles learned how to drive themselves
To our supermarkets, where the shelves
Would be restocked as soon as they went bare.
In those days, our lives were free of care;
Though limbs and organs may have atrophied,
None of us ever suffered from a need
That went unanswered by some prompt device;
Our refrigerators made their own ice!

Now, in the absence of all that, we crave,
As we'd been taught to. Some of us still wave
Those plastic cards we used to buy our stuff,
When all we had was never quite enough.
Useless, though we crave still—not what we've bought,
No, never that. That gets no further thought.

OCTAVES OF ANOTHER EDEN

1/

Nothing in their world had an origin,
Or could be thought of as original.
They called the animals their next of kin,
Though there was hardly any need to call,
So little of importance happened, ever:
Shattered plates, stains on the upholstery
Made them aware, somewhat, of entropy:
"A second-hand shop was their first endeavor..."

2/

Either they did without or else made do
With tools and clothing that required mending,
For in this garden there was nothing new,
And time went on without a thought of ending.
Once, though, she pried a rock up to uncover
A serpent who'd been dozing underneath;
He taught her how to weave a floral wreath,
And told her she was beautiful and clever.

3/

The thieves who broke into the treasury
Were amateurs, and in their bungled theft
Did many kinds of mischief; as you see
There's only one unbroken tablet left:
Pride led them to transgressions with[out num]ber,
It reads, "*Until he drove them through the gate,*

Forbidding their return to the estate.
Cast out, they fell into a dream-filled slumber."

4/
And they, when they had shaken off the spell,
Surmised their story was already known
To all those who were seated round the well
Of the amphitheater built out of the stone
Salvaged from the Wall, where it lay broken—
That ancient wonder, raised by God-knows-who,
Its fame (and theirs) refreshed now in a new
Translation from a tongue no longer spoken.

FROM CERTAIN FOOTPRINTS FOUND AT LAETOLI

1/

We may imagine they still stroll along,
Singing, perhaps, their wordless little song,

The female smaller, maybe, than the male,
And yet another with them on the trail

That leads them either to, or back from, water.
The child, who may be this pair's son or daughter,

As though to measure up to herself grown,
Steps into footprints that are not her own.

Their tracks, laid down three million years ago,
Abruptly end in eighty feet or so,

The record of their outing being kept
By the volcanic ash in which they stepped,

Heel before toe, as they went on their way,
Doing what they might do on any day.

And if the course they chose wanted correction?
Their path extends in only one direction.

2/
Their path extends in only one direction,
And etched into its interrupted section

Are indications by which we discover
Sizes and shapes, lengths of stride, whatever

Aspects successive footprints may reveal:
A depression in the far side of a heel

Shows that the female carries extra weight
On one hip, altering her normal gait:

What but an infant can be made of this?
—And then, abruptly, something seems amiss:

She halts, pauses, and turns left: does she sense
A difference that makes a difference?

Her momentary doubt is one we share
(Though without knowing what has stopped her there)

Till she continues. We watch while they recede
Before us now as signs we've learned to read.

3/
Before us now, as signs we've learned to read
Into and out of (it is they who lead

And we who follow) haltingly, to trace
The lineaments of their unhurried pace,

Our feet stumbling as theirs impress
The warm ash with recovered carelessness,

Heel before toe, heel before toe, until
The trail is discontinued: *nada, nil*—

Since they were there once, once almost in sight,
If not quite ever there, no, ever not quite,

We may imagine that these four continue
At the same pace on to another venue;

And at that moment they all disappear,
And what is left of them found only here

On the path they ventured out upon and quit
As soon as their footsteps had created it.

4/
As soon as their footsteps had created it,
Rain and another ashfall on the site

Turned into muck that turned into cement
And made their casual passage permanent

In printed code that no one had an eye for,
Or mind, until much later, to decipher.

So could the path be said then to exist?
—Not till a young paleontologist,

Out of a welter of competing spoors
(Hyenas, wildcats, rhinos, and wild boars)

Saw, in apparent isolation, what
Could only be the print of someone's foot,

And then a set of footprints that extended
For eighty feet till suddenly it ended

(And with it closed off what had been revealed)
At the beginning of another field.

5/
At the beginning of another field,
Behind him, the female burdened with a child,

And at his feet, the one who sometimes tries
His footprints on for size,

Impatient to get on with it, instead
Of waiting while he probes what lies ahead

For any sign of a better-than-even chance,
The odd turn that will favor their advance,

Some reassurance I cannot imagine.
Whether or not a counter-sign is given,

They must soon realize that if they linger
Here, they will put their issue into danger;

From now on unrecorded in the dust,
The four of them will go forth as they must,

And then (if not before) will slip out from
Whatever I can say for sure about them.

6/
Whatever I can say for sure about them,
We, like as not, would not be here without them,

Without their having set out on their way
At a certain hour of a certain day

Some three and one-half million years ago
On a quest whose purpose we can never know

That brought them here, where, without meaning to,
They left some traces of their passing through.

These traces I have come upon and made
Much of, and if my much-making has strayed

From whatever in the future comes to be
Thought to have happened, no apology,

For errors inescapably are us:
(The certainty that starts life as a guess,

The accidents that generate the plot)
We wouldn't be quite human, were they not.

7/

We wouldn't be quite human, were they not,
However small and far away, one dot

In a row of dots that, when connected, shows
A line, a path, a trail of steps that goes

From there to here, by which we may infer
We are what has become of what they were,

As they have been an early state of us
On a path once broken, now continuous.

We may imagine them, their walk begun
One terrifying morning when the sun

Was hidden in a cloud of ash and soot,
And how they had to walk completely through it

Until, quite suddenly, it all came clear,
And as they walked on slowly, with less fear,

The smaller one took up their wordless song.
We may imagine they still stroll along.

14

VARIATIONS ON A THEME BY MARTIAL

For X. J. Kennedy

Faenius, grieving, consecrates the grove
And field surrounding this new sepulcher
To Antulla, whom he will always love.
Their daughter's parents will rejoin her here
In this dear place. If you would have it, know
That those it serves will never let it go.

—*Epigrams, Book I, CXVI*

1/

"A Christian, as it happened. No, his wife,
But under torture, he confessed, to spare
Their pretty son. We let him buy that life
By making the Emperor his only heir.
Boy's in a Spanish mine. His parents made
A brilliant show on Nero's promenade."

2/

"The fortune that I spent to entertain
That imbecile reclining at my table
("More peacock tongue? Do try the monkey brain...")
Came back as the bad penny in the fable:
Five worthless acres in the Sabine Hills.
His 'gift' to me. How will I pay my bills?"

3/

"A madman who came here by accident
And without any other place to go,
Shared quarters with the tomb's sole resident

15

Until he starved to death? Perhaps, although
I have another thought: they say the one
Who built this for his daughter had a son..."

4/
"Alaric wants the vineyard where the slope's
A little less uneven. Let's begin
With clearing off the field. Right in that copse,
There's an old tomb whose roof has fallen in.
Sure, it's been looted—but just keep in mind
I get a cut of anything you find."

5/
"Each died of wounds inflicted by the other
At nearly the same time: and who knows whether
The two of them cried out to the same mother,
Were strangers or old foes who'd come together
Briefly to let a trial by arms decide
Between them for a plot of land, a bride?"

6/
"The topmost layer is a neat, long row
Of hostages, brought here in trucks and vans
Along the dirt road from the town below,
After an action by the partisans.
Machine gun bullets scarred the low stone wall.
We haven't gone down very far at all."

7/
We live upon the surface, as did they.
What lies below is largely unexplored;

Old stuff that only gets in our way
Is best forgotten, or at least ignored
As we make our way around a fertile star
On our inheritance, this abattoir.

8/
"My cousin'll take care of it for you,
And I can promise it'll cost much less
Than months without your licenses would do.
Da Faenio's expanding! You don't need stress,
You need a newer, larger parking lot,
So let the dead bury the dead—or not!"

THE LAST RESORT OF MR. KEES

"A wind that ushers winter chills the beach..."

The Funhouse had closed down the day before,
And Kees was saying with a weary sigh,
"It wasn't all that much fun, anymore."

So what, I wondered, had he gone there for,
And what, if not a weak economy,
Had closed the Funhouse down the day before?

Kees said, "We'd simply lost that old rapport
We had, once, with obstacles. As time went by
They weren't all that much fun, anymore."

Still, he seemed disappointed by the shore,
Whispering into empty seashells, "Why
Had the Funhouse closed down the day before?"

Nostalgia will demand that we restore
The laffs, the boffo gags, the hokey *schrei*,
Which aren't all that much fun, anymore.

Did I see Kees outside the Funhouse door,
Holding a sign that read, "THE END IS NIGH"?
The Funhouse had closed down the day before;
There isn't all that much fun, anymore.

MR. KEES GOES TO A PARTY

The Wilsons had just moved back into town
From summering on Wellfleet's Money Hill;
Edmund was in a very grumpy mood,
And Ann, who hadn't ever met before
The author of *Axel's Castle* and much else,
Was shocked a little by his crabbiness.
       There were two people whose names I didn't
              catch
(It turned out one of them was Philip Rice
Of the *Kenyon Review*); I spent half an hour
Trying to figure out just who they were.
Wilson repeatedly called Philip Rice
"Mr. Wheelwright." Unable to surmount
His own confusion, he demanded,
"You *are* Philip Wheelwright, are you not?"
Which may be why Rice asked me, *sotto voce*,
"Is everybody crazy in New York?"
       Mary McCarthy was busily explaining
Who the real heroine of *The Golden Bowl* is,
While Natalie Rahv told me what all was wrong
With Dwight Macdonald, and an argument
Broke out behind me over the correct
Pronunciation of Randall Jarrell's last name.
Wilson burst out with, "Accent on the last
Syllable!" adding that Jarrell was just
"An adolescent whose infantile obsessions
Were all that made his poetry worth reading."

The Wilsons left the party before we did.
We left with Rice and the man whose name I'd missed,
Although I'd somehow learned he lived and taught
In Philadelphia. I asked him what he taught.
"Until this spring I used to be the head
Of Romance Languages at Haverford;
My wife was four months pregnant with our first
Baby and then she shot herself one day."

Now he spends Tuesday evenings with Auden.
It seems that Auden's in a bad way too:
Isherwood's off in Hollywood, translating
The *Gita* with his Guru, who's a Swami,
But what he really wants to do, of course,
Is to write a novel about Hollywood.

"Christopher," said our new, still nameless friend,
"Was fascinated by *The Last Tycoon*."

NARCISSISM FOR BEGINNERS

When I first looked in on what was looking out
From the pond's surface while lying on my pier,
I only saw what I could not live without.

> *Nothing is harder than to seem sincere;*
> *Nevertheless, I most sincerely doubt*
> *That I could be other than as I appear.*

The lower lip that plumped up into a pout
Was my undoing—that, and his not-quite leer,
When I first looked in on what was looking out.

> *Until an autumn when the pond is sere,*
> *I must be always ready to put out;*
> *Nothing is harder than to seem sincere.*

There's not a moment when I don't think about
That moment when I whispered in his ear,
"I have just seen what I cannot live without."

> *I often wish, hearing him draw near,*
> *That I could have crossed eyes or a pig's snout,*
> *So I could be other than as I appear.*

This is my love, although it dare not shout
Its name or speak it, even; that much was made clear
When I first looked in on what was looking out.

Is he my slave then, or my overseer?
Some kind of genius, or a common lout?
Nothing is harder than to seem sincere.

Others learned early, and so they knew throughout
Their lives what they must cherish and revere:
But I've just seen what I could not live without.

Perhaps, as he thinks, he is just as dear
To me as I to him, I as devout:
How could I be other than as I appear?

I've lived beside the waters and known drought;
My thirst was once sated with a single tear
When I first looked in on what was looking out
And only saw what I could not live without.

So long as he looks down, I will be here.
A tear dropped in and made a waterspout!
Nothing is harder than to seem sincere.
I could be other than as I appear.

LETTER FROM KOMAROVO, 1962

Anna Akhmatova is speaking

Two opposites, each in a wicker chair,
Grandfather Frost and I: could our nations
Not have produced a less unlikely pair
Of poets unlike in their situations?

That almost sounds like something he would say,
Given the chance—a chance he would be given,
With all the honors that have come his way.
—Did he imagine that I really live in

The dacha where he found me? Or understand
What my life has been like? Wasn't it clear
That our meeting had been wholly planned
By those in charge? Could I have said,

                                   "My dear,
You are your president's honor-laden guest,
The apple picker picking one last apple
Before you sleep. My writing was suppressed,
While yours received all that a grateful people

Could offer up to someone not yet dead:
All fame, all glory, accolades, distinction!
My poems cling to their lives by the thread
Of memory, fraying toward the extinction

They've been rehearsing as the years went by,
When no one was allowed even to mention
My name in print, and my poems and I
Cooperated to avoid attention.

Some still exist, others have been burned
By 'the responsible organs of the state,' or
Were copied out and given to be learned
By those who could be executed, later.

You've always had the freedom to make free,
And yet you write, as though somehow you hadn't:
'The strong are saying nothing till they see.'
But over here the strong are always prudent,

For long ago the strong learned not to speak
Until the strongest raised his hand and voted.
Theirs is a concentration that the weak,
Whose speech may be ignored as it is noted,

Can somehow never manage to achieve.
The weak are free in their own estimation
And may smile back at smiles meant to deceive,
Or note the censure in the long ovation...

But here we are, two poets of our time,
Each one a cipher, really, to the other.
Two old people, practitioners of rhyme,
Sitting in our wicker chairs together—

Perhaps we're not that unalike at all:
The curtain that so long ago ascended
On our age is now about to fall
After the toasts and banquets have all ended..."

It's said that we are both up for the Prize.
Let him have it, then: my doctors have forbidden
Me to travel—my health, you see!
                              They advise
Especially against a trip to Sweden.

"*NOI ANTRI*": Three Poems from the Romanesco of G. G. Belli

1/ The Sovrans of the Old World

So there's this King, that once upon a time
Sends out an edict to his huddled masses:
"Now I am I, and you're not worth a dime,
You lying beggars, so just shut your faces.

"I let you know what's crooked and what's straight,
'Cause I could sell you all off by the lot,
Or if I went and hanged you all—so what?
Your lives and stuff belong to me, the state.

"The one without a title to his name,
Who isn't King, or Emperor, or Pope,
Just hasn't got the cards to play the game."

And with this edict comes a hangman who
Says, "Whaddaya think?" while dandling his rope,
And all of them reply, "That's true! That's true!"

2/ A Dog's Life

You call this *idleness*, you idiots?
You say the Pope does *nothing*? *Nothing*, eh?
Goddam you for belittling the way
He labors through the grueling days and nights.

Who speaks to God Almighty in his chapel?
Who pardons whoreson rogues for their offenses?
Who sends out barrels of indulgences?
Who blesses, from his limousine, the people?

Who counts the little coins up of his pelf?
Who helps him with the cardinals he invests?
Who else may levy taxes but himself?

And what of the fatigue that must set in
From tearing up petitions and requests
And tossing all those scraps into the bin?

3/ The Confessor

"*Father?*" "Begin with the Confiteor."
"*I did.*" "Act of Contrition?" "*Yes.*" "Commence."
"*I called my husband dickbrain.*" "Is there more?"
"*I stole from him a dollar fifty cents.*"

"What else?" "*When Pussy broke a pot, I said,*
I was so angry with her, 'Go to hell!'
And she's God's creature!" "Are we done yet?"

                                                    "*Well...*
There's this young fellow that I took to bed."

"What happened then?" "*Some in and out and in...*"
"But always in the...designated place?"
"*And in the one behind it.*" "O beastly sin!

"And so because of your young reprobate,
Come with repentant heart and downcast face
Tomorrow, daughter, my house, around eight."

THE WOMAN TAKEN IN ADULTERY

John 7:53–8:11

And how would *I* know what the Master said?
There was a mob of fools surrounding me,
The very ones that dragged me from my bed
Yammering on about adultery—
Who turned me in? The one-eyed Pharisee,
A loathsome little hypocrite, hell-bent
On vengeance for not getting past my knee,
If you catch my drift.
                         The others only meant
To trap the Master in an argument
So dangerous that he'd have no retort.
He must have won, though: silenced, off they went,
And him left sitting in the temple court
Where, with one finger in the dust, he traced
Odd little squiggles that he soon erased.

THE LOCKED-ROOM MYSTERY
OF MR. KEES

For John T. Irwin

Traditionally, there are only two
Possible solutions: suicide or murder.
That knife in the back says, "It's no suicide!"
But no one other than the corpse is present;
Doors and windows are all locked from within.
Mr. Kees takes all this in, in silence,

But wonders, why would someone want to silence
A figure so marginal? It appears that two
Passersby heard screaming from within
The locked-room mystery, "Like bloody murder!"
Mr. Kees is not impressed. "At present,
I don't think we can rule out suicide;

Tell you the truth, I lean toward suicide,"
Says Mr. Kees. There is an awkward silence,
Which empty speech balloons would represent
In a comic strip. "But I've known one or two
Suicides who made it look like murder,
By messing with the door locks from within;

It had to do, as I recall now, with in-
surance," says Mr. Kees. "A suicide
Takes less dissimulation than a murder."
His eyes are closed. The count begins: *One...two...*

Three, and he leans forward into the silence
Of time reduced to an eternal present...

Rehearsing, just! The void is not yet present,
Though he has often felt it stir within;
"Yes, this is Mr. Kees. Sunday at two?
I'd love to, but I've got this suicide
I have to solve—" At the other end, shocked silence.
"I'm sorry, Mrs. Morse—I mean, a murder."

"How thrilling! Mr. Kees will solve a murder!
Is that the reason why he isn't present?"
But Mrs. Morse has sworn her guests to silence:
"If this conundrum isn't cleft within
The next few hours, it's his suicide.
Let's see, now: it's already half past two."

He's gone: a murder? No: clues found within
His rooms present the case for suicide.
One dines in silence at a table set for two.

A HAPPY ENDING FOR *IPHIS*
AND *IANTHE*

*After Ovid, Metamorphoses, Book IX, ll. 666–797; with
reference to Oxyrinchus Papyrus 744*

Written two thousand years ago or better,
Then tossed away on a papyrus heap
Where it lay buried until now, this letter
From a trader peddling clay pots or sheep
Instructs his pregnant wife, lest she forget her
Maternal duties: "Know that you may keep
The child, if it's a boy; if not a son,
Well then, my dear, you know what must be done."

Of course she does, for any woman knows it,
Even if she's not told, "Use common sense:
We can't afford so much as the deposit
On a dowry's impossible expense!"
And so she must give up a girl, expose it
To wild dogs and the wilder elements.
Unless... *Unless?* "There's no alternative:
We're just too poor to let a daughter live..."

So *Ligdus* to his woman, *Telethusa*,
Who alternates between self-hating rage
And cursing out her husband. It's no use: a
Grief arises in her she cannot assuage—
What do men know of childbirth? How profuse a
Shower of tears rains down upon that page,
Because of his implacable decision!
That evening, in bed, though, came a vision:

32

Before her stood the shining goddess, *Isis*,
Surrounded by the members of her court,
In full regalia: had *Telethusa's* crisis
Summoned the goddess hither? Yes, in short.
(I often find a summary suffices,
Where others might include the full report.)
For *Isis* came just as her water broke,
And as the woman gasped, the goddess spoke,

And what she said made *Telethusa* shiver:
"Ignore your husband! Listen just to me,
And when your time is come and you deliver,
Accept your child, whatever it may be,
And bring it up. Don't sell it down the river,
Or toss it on the midden, heartlessly.
If you obey me, you will not complain
That money spent on me was spent in vain."

She swore obedience to her defender,
And in due time, and all quite painlessly,
She had a girl, and to conceal its gender,
The nurse was told to "feed my boy." Secrecy
Attended the swaddling of the wee pretender,
Whose nurse and mother always called it "he."
Ligdus, with a male heir now, knew bliss,
And did not think or guess aught was amiss;

Her father named her *Iphis* (my italics),
A boy's name that was used by girls as well,
Like *Tracy* or like *Jordan* or like *Alex*.
(You may remember *"Pat"* from SNL.)

One wonders though, about the . . . well, the phallic S-
ituation: was there no show and tell?
Did *Ligdus* never go along with "him"
For an outing at the bathhouse or the gym?

Deception started small, and the unwary
Were taken by it as it grew and grew,
As *Iphis* did. The swift years do not tarry:
Her parents realize what they must do.
At thirteen, they arrange for her to marry
The girl next door, *Ianthe*, whom she knew,
Of course, a girl as beautiful as she.
Both hearts are warmed by first love equally,

Although each has a different expectation:
Ianthe is inclined now to entwine,
Iphis feels a gnawing desperation:
"There is a flaw in nature's grand design,
Which I embody! Where in all creation
Is there another case as strange as mine?"
Poor *Iphis* cries. "A maid who loves a maid!
How very singular I am," she said.

"Oh, what will be the end reserved for *Iphis*,
Gripped by such odd, indecent feelings known
To no one else? Far sharper than a knife is
This passion that cuts right through to the bone,
But leaves me with the loneliness my life is,
Weeping like *Niobe*, transformed into stone,
Doomed like *Oedipus*—will I get my own complex
For loving someone of the selfsame sex?"

But it wasn't just the global implications,
Her fear that there was no one anywhere
Like her at all among the teeming nations,
No other girl with whom she'd ever share
Her woes and sorrows, transports and elations,
That added on as much to her despair
As thinking of her sure embarrassment
When festive wedding torches lay all spent;

She had to know that a first night's inspection,
Tender but pressing, would at once reveal
The source of the unnatural affection
She had so long attempted to conceal;
There was no way that she could rise to action
And give *Ianthe* proof her love was real;
She, on her part, found it hard to wait
While *Iphis* kept on pushing back the date

With one concocted pretext and another,
Until the day had dawned, and what to do?
It suddenly occurred to *Iphis*'s mother
To call again upon that goddess who
Had helped them when they were in such a pother,
And see if she would once again come through—
—Fervent prayers, rich offerings were made
To *Isis*, who, of course, provided aid,

And her solution proved to be quite simple,
For *Iphis* was transformed into a lad
While following his mother from the temple.
Those two were pleased; *Ianthe* too was glad,

Who noticed on his chin a lovely dimple
She could have sworn that he had never had
Before—a charm she would explore at leisure,
When the time came, as it soon would, for pleasure.

With *Ovid* as her aider and abettor,
Isis now has the talent to provide
A happy ending whereby she'll enfetter
Iphis, who stands in manly garb beside
Ianthe, beaming, in a skirt and sweater,
The rescue bridegroom and his grateful bride;
The goddess with her friends, and everyone
All thanking her for everything she's done!

Leave *Iphis* and *Ianthe* in their bower
For now, as we assume that presently
Her virtue will surrender to his power;
And that, by morning, passersby will see
The proof that there was something to deflower
In dappled bedsheets on the balcony.
We'll keep our own misgivings to ourselves,
Or try to—but the modern spirit delves:

How can the fix of godly intervention
Provide us more than comical relief?
These days it requires the suspension
Of almost everybody's disbelief
In the miraculous—not to mention
The way in which the ending scants that grief
Which, after all, was the reality:
A girl put out to die would either die,

Or else be taken up by an enslaver,
And spend her little life in paying down
That debt to which *Death* only grants a waiver.
She was between a hard place and a stone,
And nothing but a miracle could save her;
But *Ovid*'s miracles are never shown
To ordinary folk of *Iphis*'s kind:
I mean real girls in a real sort of bind—

Undying *Sibyl* goes from old to older,
Medusa now has snakes instead of hair;
Niobe has been turned into a boulder,
The nymph *Callisto* is a shaggy bear;
When *Daphne* gave *Apollo* the cold shoulder,
She found herself become a laurel; there
Are cases very similar, yet these
Are all immortal singularities,

Whose transformations are involuntary
And always meant to frighten and appall
With consequences which, of course, will vary;
And though they entertain us and enthrall,
The endings are unpleasant, even scary—
But *happy* endings? There are none at all.
Yet *Ovid* goes along with happiness,
Will settle, so it seems, for nothing less.

Why couldn't our pair just live together
In sin or bliss, quite happily unwed,
Or, for that matter, wed, no matter whether
Two girls, two boys, two something else instead;

Be *Jordan* and *Tracy* with the little *Heather*
They've rescued from the city of the dead,
And after several days of celebration,
They are now raising as their very own?

We are more used to wandering in chartless
Regions than was our *Ovid* in his time,
But it's the goddess who in fact proves heartless
In her devotion to the cold sublime;
And it's our poet, our far from artless
Ironist, who reveals the paradigm
Of human freedom we still struggle toward.
And even though he won't have the last word,

He'd move us past all deities descending
In their spectacular machinery,
No matter what they may have been intending;
He'd find that broken space where irony
Helps us to evade an imposed ending,
A happy ending, most especially.
Give *Isis* the last word or she'll be vexed.

Let *Ovid* have whatever word comes next.

MR. KEES COMES TO A CONCLUSION

This is the secret guessed by Mr. Kees:
There was no letter waiting to be sent,
And that is all: there are no mysteries,

Only the parents he could never please,
And a clear bottle labeled PUNISHMENT;
This is the secret guessed by Mr. Kees:

Though he should beg for pardon on his knees,
There was a silence that would not relent,
And that is all: there were no mysteries

About the young man who seemed ill at ease,
And what his furtive gestures may have meant;
This is the secret guessed by Mr. Kees:

There was a light that flickered in the trees
Which once seemed meaningful in its intent,
And that is all: there are no mysteries.

All locks will be sprung open by their keys,
There is no hour that will not be spent;
This is the secret guessed by Mr. Kees,
And that is all. There are no mysteries.

BLUE EYES

After Octavio Paz

You know what those provincial towns are like: just one
  hotel,
And just one restaurant where you can get a decent meal.
And nothing after that to do but stroll around the square
Watching the locals watching you till boredom or despair
Drives you back to your room. I got in shortly before dark,
Unpacked my samples, freshened up. Downstairs, the hotel
  clerk
Mentioned a café he liked, close enough to walk to.
The usual, but clean, and with a waitress there to talk to,
A young girl, pretty and flirtatious: shortly it appeared
The night might not be quite as uneventful as I'd feared.
I had a brandy after dinner, smoked a cigarette,
Then someone outside called to her and, beaming, my
  coquette
Took off her apron and took off at once: end of story.
      So, with no prospects for the night, a busy day
        before me,
I saw that it was time for me to pack it in: retread
The path that I had taken here back to my room and bed.
But all the shops along the streets were shuttered for the
  night,
And as I might have known, there was no other source of
  light.
I set out walking blindly then, went on and on until
I realized that I was lost, stopped walking and stood still.

The footsteps I'd been hearing abruptly stopped when
     mine did.
I felt that I'd been drawn into a labyrinth that winded
Inward, in response to my confusion and distress.
     And then, as I was passing by a shadowy recess,
I caught a glimpse of some slight movement in that
     cul-de-sac,
And someone seized me from behind: while one hand drew
     me back
Into the deeper darkness there, the other calmly brought
The pressure of a cold steel blade hard against my throat.
     "Be careful now, don't move," he said. "I have a razor
     here,
And men will sometimes choose unwisely, on account of
     fear."
I said, "My wallet's in…" He said, "You don't quite
     comprehend:
Your wallet isn't what I want from you, tonight, my friend;
It isn't all that simple. I can only wish it were.
My woman asks me for this, and I do it to please her.
For she has told me that she wants—imagine my surprise!
Tomorrow, for her birthday, a bouquet of eyes, blue eyes,
Yes, they must all of them be blue." I couldn't answer him:
The thought of losing both my eyes to satisfy a whim!
     "That is the only reason why I've interrupted you:
I have to have your eyes tonight, my friend, if they are blue."
     "My eyes are not…that color," I said. "Look! They are
     dark brown."
He took the razor from my throat, but didn't put it down.
"Matches," he said, and, "Light one now." I heeded his
     command.

The cardboard box was rattling in my unsteady hand
So fiercely that I dropped the flaring match. "Again," he said.
And so I struck another match that flared up like my dread:
"Now hold it closer to your eyes, hold up that little torch!"
I held it up until I felt my lashes start to scorch.
The match had burned down to my fingers when he blew
    it out.
"I should have trusted you, my friend. Can you forgive my
    doubt?"
He let me go, and in a moment he had disappeared.
    I fell back into darkness, but not blind, as I had feared,
And still alive, or so it seemed. For a long time I lay
In shock, until I managed to get up and make my way
Back to the hotel, and next morning, packed, and fled that
    place,
Driving as swiftly as I could away from my disgrace.
    You realize that I had lied to him? My eyes *are* blue.
Did he miss that? The flaring match? How can I know if
    he knew?
It's possible he only meant to test me, I suppose.
But did I pass or fail that test? Who else but that man
    knows?

THE AFTERLIFE OF MR. KEES

*"The phone rang. One of the policemen answered. Then
he put the handset down on the cradle and told the others
that no one had been on the other end."*

The phone was ringing and to make it stop
He answered it. Not what you might expect:
"It wasn't nobody," announced the cop.

Friends of his said that Kees seemed full of hope
Two days before: did none of them suspect?
The phone kept ringing and it wouldn't stop

Repeating its summons to adjust and cope,
Even as Kees made plans to disconnect.
"It wasn't nobody," announced the cop,

Who yesterday had missed Kees poised atop
The polished railing, momently erect:
A phone was ringing and Kees made it stop

By tilting forward till he began to drop
From a vertiginous sheer height, unchecked.
"It wasn't nobody," announced the cop.

Waves still spread out from Kees's great belly-flop
At frequencies now harder to detect,
A phone that rings unheard and will not stop.
"It wasn't nobody," announced the cop.

TWO

THE MESSENGER'S SPEECH FROM EURIPIDES' *MEDEA*

> *Medea has sent her children off with poisoned gifts for Jason's new bride, Creon's daughter, and is anxiously awaiting news of their reception, when she sees the Messenger approaching.*

MEDEA:
My friends, I have been waiting in suspense
For a long time, to see what would ensue!
—Now one of Jason's men comes into view,
Gasping for breath! No doubt to announce
Some gratifying new catastrophe!

> *Messenger enters from stage right.*

MESSENGER: *(Gasping)*
Your lawless act's resulted in disaster,
Medea! Go NOW! You've no choice but to flee
By ship or chariot, whichever's faster!

MEDEA: *(Calmly)*
Why must I hasten? What is happening?

MESSENGER:
You've poisoned both the Princess and King Creon!

MEDEA:
—You'll be my cherished friend from this day on,
So splendid a report it is you bring!

MESSENGER: *(Puzzled)*
You can't be all there, lady. Are you mad?
You've just destroyed the royal family
And you joke about it? Aren't you afraid?

MEDEA:
Words, words. Oh, if I wished, I could reply...
But slow down, friend: I mean to savor this.
Now tell me—since you saw it: How did they die?
In agony? Then I'll have twice the bliss!

MESSENGER:
When your two boys and husband had appeared
At the bride's house and entered, those of us who
Had suffered from your griefs were greatly cheered:
From ear to ear, the welcome news that you
Had settled amicably with your spouse
Went buzzing through the servants of the house.
One kissed the children's hands in his elation,
Another, their golden curls. I shared in their joys
And followed the swelling throng in celebration
Into the women's quarters with your boys.
    The mistress we now honor in your place
Wasn't aware your sons were there at first—
Her gaze was fixed on her new husband's face,
And the boys' approach took her by surprise.
Soon as she noticed them, she veiled her eyes
And turned away her pale cheek in disgust.
    Your husband, though, attempted to assuage
Her anger, telling her, "You mustn't be
An enemy of those who are dear to me;

Turn back to us again, without your rage,
Let those I call my friends be yours as well;
They bring you gifts, which I would have you take—
Then plead with Creon so he won't expel
The children from this land—for your husband's sake!"

     As soon as she had seen the elegant
Finery they offered, all resistance
Collapsed, and she gave Jason her consent.
He and the boys had travelled no great distance
From the bride's house, when she put on the gown,
And on her golden curls set the gold crown,
As pleased as any girl by a new bonnet.
She held a mirror up before her hair,
Smiled at the lifeless image glimpsed within it,
Then lifted herself lightly from her chair
And elegantly danced about her suite,
Rapt in her gifts, admiring them
And how they suited her: her pale white feet
Capering as she checked her swirling hem.

     Then came a truly horrifying sight:
Her color changed, she staggered left and right
Stumbling until she found her seat once more,
Managing, barely, to avoid the floor!
One of her slaves, perhaps in the belief
That she had either been possessed by Pan
Or by another god, raised a festive cry—
Until she saw the white foam on her lips,
And the tormented madness in her eye,
Her bloodless skin—the hymn that she began
Trailed off and turned into a wail of grief.

     At once a servant ran to find her father

Back in his chambers, as yet unaware
Of what had just been happening—another
Went searching for the husband, now outside,
To tell him what had happened to his bride;
Others were running madly everywhere.

      In the time in which a rapid sprinter runs
The second leg of a two hundred yard dash,
The princess became conscious once again.
Her eyes sprang open and she groaned in pain,
For grief assailed her from two sources now,
As suddenly a dreadful stream of flame
Erupted from the garland on her brow,
While the woven robe, the gift of your two sons,
Was eating through the wretched woman's flesh.

      Then leaping from her chair, she fled, on fire,
Tossing her hair now one way, now another,
Trying to shake the garland from her head,
But the golden band shook off *her* instead,
And her exertions made the flames leap higher!
Disaster claimed her. She crumpled to the floor,
Unrecognizable but to a father:
Her eyes no longer lovely, as before,
That face of hers no longer beautiful.
Fiery blood dripped from her ruined crown,
And from her white bones the scorched flesh fell
Like resin from a pine torch dripping down
All burned off by the poisons you'd employed.
No one could bear to see the girl destroyed,
Yet none was brave enough to intervene,
So well had we all learned from what we'd seen.

      But when her father, who had not yet heard

Of the calamity that had occurred,
Came in and stumbled on her without warning,
He clasped her body in a last embrace,
And as he kissed her desolated face,
Maddened by grief, cried out these words of mourning:
"O my unlucky darling, my poor dear,
Which of the gods has treated you this way,
Has shamed you like this on your wedding day?
I am bereft, a walking sepulcher!
O daughter, daughter, let me die with you!"
But when his lamentation had at last
Ended and the king attempted to
Lift his aged body to his feet once more,
He found himself stuck to the gown, held fast
By the subtle stuff that drew him toward the floor,
Clinging to him as ivy clings to bay.
He struggled, but he couldn't get away:
She held him and prevented him from rising,
And if he struggled with her, it would flense
The ancient flesh from his unyielding bones.
That was enough. Enough to say that he
Died, overwhelmed by his catastrophe.
Who would not weep? They lie there side by side
In death, an agèd father, a young bride.

   I will say nothing of *your* likely fate,
But soon enough, you'll get your recompense.
I've often thought that life is just a show
Of shadows, and I wouldn't hesitate
To say that those most sure of what they know,
Whose polished speeches reek of confidence,
Are the more fools to think themselves clever!

Turns from Medea to address the
audience directly:
No mortal may attain to a blessèd state:
If wealth pours in, you're truly fortunate,
You're lucky in your life. But blessèd? Never.
Exit Messenger from stage right.

THREE

A CHILD OF THE FUTURE PERFECT

A Sonnet Sequence

1/

My parents had been born into the past,
Which suited them, I think you'd have to say.
The Great Depression shaken off at last,
They stepped into an ancient Model A
(My mother's father's gift) and drove away.
Not very far: They'd shortly disembark
To live in line with Le Corbusier:
His high-rise towers in a verdant park
Were copied in—Why not?—the Bronx, New York.
"Geometries of joy and light and air"
Created something that was wholly new
And clueless as to how it ought to work.
It was called Parkchester, and it was where
I would be born in 1942.

2/

For Wallace Stevens, that transcendent scribe,
We live in the ideas about a place,
Not the place itself. If I try to describe
This "rationally formulated space
Consisting of four quadrants which embrace
An oval pool where piscine sculptures spout,
Towers of varied height and red brick face—"
See what I mean? Of all the ideas about,
"Security within, peril without,"
Was probably the most important one,
For its imperative must be obeyed.
What could go wrong when evil forces flout
The rules of order that are soon undone?
A Little Golden Book of mine displayed

3/

The savagery that lies outside the law:
How easily did Wolf—so bad, so big,
Blow down the foolish First Pig's house of straw,
Then move on to destroy the house of twig
Erected, so to speak, by Second Pig.
Wolf was defeated by Third Pig, whose lair
Was built of brick—like Parkchester, you dig?
A Nazi was that Wolf, whose character
And principles would be replaced by Bear
In a Cossack hat that must have kept him warm.
Bear's taste for honey led him to the hive,
Whose occupants took to the upper air
And drove him off with their fierce buzzing swarm;
"Children, it's thanks to them you're still alive."

4/

Such parables of economic ruin
And foreigners hell-bent on violence
In tales of Wolf & Pig, of Bee & Bruin,
Were given us to show by inference
That practicality and common sense
(And dwelling in impregnable brick towers)
Created a not-to-be-sneezed-at defense
Against the ogre outside who devours.
Exclusion, it may be, is what empowers:
Should we meet Wolf or Bear in a dark wood,
What shielded us before now disappears;
But roller skating on the street for hours,
We had the freedom of the neighborhood,
Oblivious to our parents' fears.

5/

I grew up where the future came to pass
In a kind of corporate experiment:
The towers set on islands of mown grass
Beckoned, affordable: *O come and rent!*
My parents moved like nomads from a tent
Into a city newly occupied,
A way of living without precedent.
What was the present but the past denied?
The residents had little else beside
A past with all its axes left to grind,
Owing to the hard times they'd gone through.
But here they were now, and so now they tried
To get ahead, keep up, not fall behind,
Since now they had what to look forward to:

6/

A future bought on the installment plan
That seemed to offer never less than more—
The coffee table and the plush divan
Spilled from its lavish cornucopia.
The first installments were of furniture,
Appliances: a snapshot would reveal
My mother and me at curbside waiting for
My father to appear behind the wheel
Of a 1947 Oldsmobile
Sedan, as cozy as our living room.
They might have asked if their success was real,
But must have thought it proper to assume
That they deserved it to go on and on,
That God and a brand-new Frigidaire were one...

7/

Like Buck Rogers in the 25th Century,
I was convinced that what had been foretold
Would be delivered, for much certainty
Attended each prediction: soon jet-propelled
Backpacks would be invented to uphold
Our fathers in their daily commutation
From the high brick towers in which we now dwelled
To the recently repurposed subway station
(Hardened to resist annihilation),
Wherein a single slim pneumatic tube
Would huff each passenger by automation
Into his office's pulsating cube:
A FIVE-COURSE MEAL REPLACED BY ONE SMALL PILL!
Others, I guess, await this future still,

8/

But I've been disappointed far too often
By all the IOUs my time amassed;
By how the future seemed to blur and soften
As it approached us and then skidded past
Without unloading any from its vast
Warehouse of soon-to-be's, briskly onswept
Ahead of us, and we, the overpassed,
Forever enduring promises not kept.
Until they were. But when Neil Armstrong stepped
Into the future, it at once became
Part of the past, no matter that he leapt
And gamboled in the moondust like a lamb.
On earth we peered into a boundless deep:
HUMANITY WILL OUTGROW NEED FOR SLEEP

9/

So there were futures that would be stillborn,
Others that had already taken place,
And some quite likely to: SCIENTISTS WARN
THAT [YOUR FEAR HERE] COULD END THE HUMAN RACE!
That I could vanish without any trace,
And just at the onset of puberty,
Seemed possible: a future to erase
All other futures that I might foresee.
My parents' unaddressed anxiety,
The fears they couldn't bring themselves to mention
Over what still has not yet come to be,
Had some connection with RISING COLD WAR TENSION
And in the silos where it was confined,
A certain future that got left behind.

10/

But not before the leaders of our nation
Had doubled down on their unlikely bet
That shelters would preserve our civilization.
I soon discovered, much to my regret,
That, although planned for, shelters were as yet
Unconstructed—a fact that left me feeling
Abandoned, for what succor could I get
By digging through my downstairs neighbor's ceiling?
The future opened up for me, revealing
A present tense of phones and elevators,
Indoor plumbing, polished chrome (APPEALING
TO THE HOUSEWIFE OF TODAY), refrigerators—
And in a moment, all of it dissolves!
I dreamt of boys and girls brought up by wolves...

11/

Although they fed them at their lupine feasts,
And let them snuggle in their dens at night,
These children had no future with the beasts:
They could not learn to speak or walk upright
Or think of the delicious things that might
Be theirs, if only they could master flame,
And somehow learn a word for "appetite."
They were removed when missionaries came
And baptized them (in case they hadn't been)
And gave each wolf-child a religious name
And taught them with a ruler about sin
And the economy of guilt and shame
And at what great a distance they'd been cursed.
But could their situation be reversed?

12/

Begin with children, all attending Mass,
Who, at the clicker, drop down to their knees
And open wide: the First Communion class.
Outwardly docile, yet what mysteries
Were to be glimpsed behind their hooded eyes,
How eager some of them were to exchange
The narrow path for ungrooved wilderness,
Robes of salvation for a wolfish mange!
It wouldn't take much doing to derange
Their senses and turn certainty to doubt,
To stimulate a craving for the strange,
So much the present seems to have shut out.
I knelt down in the lightless box then, praying.
And heard a voice, distinctly other, saying,

13/

"So that was you, in the confessional
With some old priest attending some new sin,
As I tore strips of meat from a fresh kill,
Then crawled back through the thick legs crowding in,
To scarf the orphan's share—little *White Skin*,
Named for my pasty face and hairless pelt.
I danced beneath the full moon with my kin
In the primeval forest where we dwelt,
And could not stem the urges that I felt
When we collapsed in a hugger-mugger heap!
Pardon demanded kneeling, so you knelt,
While I fell into a rich phantasmal sleep
In which appeared the lurid, awkward shapes
Of my companions, the anthropoid apes.

14/

"And from that dream, I brought *procession* back,
And made my figures move with dignity,
Clothed as they were in hooded robes of black;
And let them know that impassivity,
Proscription, and obedience would be
The order of the day; and made them next
Drop to the cold stone floor on bended knee
And chant from the unalterable text
Of revelation's guide for the perplexed;
And without hesitation to proclaim
The truths I taught them and remain unvexed
In persecution and in victory the same
And on occasion to employ the knife
Sharpened to take the blameless victim's life.

15/

"For always there's a scene of someone killing
Someone chosen in another's stead;
The victim, although bound, is always willing
And doesn't ever struggle as he's led
Up to the block where he will lose his head,
Or to that stage on which he will be torn,
His gift of life compressed into a seed
That will be buried till new life is born.
His is the death you are prescribed to mourn.
No enmity at all: lift blade and strike,
No matter whether stranger or first-born,
And dip your fingers in their blood alike.
Then beg forgiveness for what has been done,
For you and your community are one—

16/
"One with your leader, one superior
To you and to the others of your kind,
Those adolescent males who cringe before
His rush, his presence, and who stoop to find
Some way to gratify their lord's behind.
He'll hold his powers only for as long
As none of you, not singly or combined
Will take him on, the strongest of the strong.
He knows that somewhere in that restless throng
There is a payback waiting to be claimed,
A retribution certain to come due:
What he took from another will belong
To someone else when he is killed or maimed
And driven off by someone in that crew

17/
"Of cast-out boys, an unrelated horde
Persuading one another to attack—
Oh, anything to keep from being bored!
—Step forward one by one and then fall back
Into the deep protection of the pack,
Until there finally emerges one
Distinguished by unmitigated lack:
Pinched, puny, hairless, upright, accident prone,
This fantasist who spends his days alone,
Is he the one who will take down the king?
Once all the cautious circling is done,
They hunker down into a crouch, then spring,
And suddenly—why, there's a flashing blade!
A cry reverberates within the glade ..."

18/
To leave such a suspenseful narrative
At this point might, to some, seem like a crime
Impossible for readers to forgive.
Others will likely mutter, "About time—
We've had enough of the Freudian Sublime,
Not to mention the Pulp Vulgarity.
Just get us out of here—turn on a dime,
And save us both from terminal ennui."
I trust by now that all of us can see
How myths spring up from our monuments
Built or projected, how the truth soon yields
To fiction as the mind's own alchemy,
At work on our daily experience,
Turns playgrounds into primal battlefields,

19/
And makes a bloodbath out of any sport,
Owing to our fierce imaginings;
Achilles rages on the handball court,
Accountants of the future exchange rings
And are translated into queens and kings
Out of the ordinary, our dialect.
Though I can break off from these ramblings,
It won't be easy now to redirect
This craft of mine: you know by now (you've checked),
That sonnets in this sequence often spin
Off from the last lines of the one before it;
So at this point I have to interject
A hasty reference to sonnet 9,
And "a future banked in silos where they store it."

20/

It's time now to revisit, if you will,
That certain future's odd uncertainty:
It hasn't happened yet, and yet it's still
Poised between "sure to come" and "not to be";
A countdown that began when I was three,
A sword that hangs above each conscious head,
Still balanced ever so improbably,
Suspended by a single, fraying, thread.
Imagine living with such conscious dread.
Yet that's how we all think now, if we think
At all about it. No matter what we were,
That future only will be inherited
By our descendants, driven to the brink
Of what, with any luck, might not occur.

21/

But there's no way to undo what we've done,
Unknow what we have known; no point decreeing
That rivers may against their currents run;
Shall we unsee what we have seen? "Unseeing"
Isn't a verb: points to a state of being
Which is our own, when every day increases
That possibility there is no fleeing,
When ire, ignorance, and our caprices
Conclude to press the button that releases
All the downtrodden demons from their lair;
And at that moment when the button's pressed
Our unflagging agitation ceases;
Not, so far, yet: not ashes on the air,
But the news, for now, that *"This has been a test..."*

22/

It was a frequent theme of cartoon humor
When I was young, the feckless moron who
Had painted himself right into a corner
Not to be lifted out of or gone through.
Above his head, the question, "What to do?"
And on his face a look of mere distress.
He had failed the test. Options? Only two:
Just sit there, or walk out and leave a mess.
The former option seems to offer less,
A minimum of praise, but far less blame:
No matter whether witting or unwitting,
Not to have blown it so far is success,
And the trees that have not yet burst into flame
May bless you for your charity in sitting.

23/

The paint that I've applied has not dried yet,
And I've begun to think it never will.
The room is darker, for the sun has set:
When the last light fades from the window sill,
The room will be completely dark until
Tomorrow's sun comes to shed light upon
The painted floor that will gleam damply still,
Letting me know my future has begun.
The still-wet floor and the recurrent sun
Are bound together indissolubly;
Resentment, envy, and self-sacrifice
Attend on the figures of my meditation,
But in the future I may come to see
How what is happening now will suffice.

FAREWELL, *VOYAGER 1*

Go seek for us—I mean, in our place,
Through vacancies of interstellar space,
And then (to teach us?) vanish without trace.

NOTES

Discontents: My source here is an epigram of Petronius from his *Satyricon*: "Inveniet quod quisque velit: non omnibus unum est / quod placet: hic spinas colligit, ille rosas." Translated by Michael Heseltine and W. H. D. Rouse, Loeb Classical Library. Harvard University Press, 1975.

From Certain Footprints Found at Laetoli: For an account of their discovery and preservation, see "The Footprints at Laetoli," by Neville Agnew and Martha Demas, in *Conservation Perspectives: The GCI Newsletter* 10.1, 1995.

The Last Resort of Mr. Kees: My epigraph is taken from Kees's poem, "Resort," in *The Collected Poems of Weldon Kees (Revised Edition)*, edited by Donald Justice, University of Nebraska Press, 1960.

Mr. Kees Goes to a Party: My source is a letter Kees wrote to Maurice Johnson, December 6, 1943, found in *Weldon Kees and the Midcentury Generation: Letters, 1935–1955*, edited by Robert E. Knoll, Bison Books, 1986.

Narcissism for Beginners: See Ovid, *Metamorphoses*, Book III, ll. 407–510.

Letter from Komarovo, 1962: Anna Akhmatova is speaking of her meeting with Robert Frost during his goodwill visit to the USSR in that year; the classic account of the visit is found in F. D. Reeve's *Robert Frost in Russia*, Little, Brown, 1963. The prize that Akhmatova refers to is the Nobel Prize for Literature, which either she or Frost were supposed to win that year. It went instead to John Steinbeck.

Blue Eyes: Homage to Octavio Paz, whose story, "The Blue Bouquet," I read, translated by Lysander Kemp, in the *Evergreen Review* (No. 18) in 1961 and never forgot.

The Afterlife of Mr. Kees: My epigraph and its context may be found in the prologue to James Reidel's biography, *Vanished Act: The Life and Art of Weldon Kees*, Bison Books, 2003.

A Child of the Future Perfect: What Wallace Stevens actually wrote, in a letter to Henry Church, on April 4, 1945, was: "It seems to me to be an interesting idea: that is to say, the idea that we live in the description of a place, and not in the place itself, and in every vital sense we do." *Letters of Wallace Stevens*, selected and edited by Holly Stevens, University of California Press, 1966.

ACKNOWLEDGMENTS

I am grateful to the editors of the following journals, in which many of the poems in this collection have previously been published, sometimes in different forms and/or with different titles: *Arion* ("Narcissism for Beginners" and "A Happy Ending for *Iphis* and *Ianthe*"), *The Birmingham Poetry Review* ("When We Had It All" and "A Child of the Future Perfect," as "The Age of Knowledge"), *The Hopkins Review* ("From Certain Footprints Found at Laetoli" and "The Locked-Room Mystery of Mr. Kees"), *The Hudson Review* ("From 'A Child of the Future Perfect'"), *Measure* ("Variations on a Theme by Martial"), *The New Criterion* ("Octaves of Another Eden"), *THINK* ("The Afterlife of Mr. Kees" and "Mr. Kees Goes To a Party"), and *The Yale Review* ("Letter From Komarovo, 1962" and "The Woman Taken in Adultery").

Charles Martin is the author of six books of poetry, including *Steal the Bacon*, *What the Darkness Proposes*, *Starting from Sleep: New and Selected Poems*, which was a finalist for the Lenore Marshall Award of the Academy of American Poets, and *Signs & Wonders*. His verse translation of Ovid's *Metamorphoses* received the 2004 Harold Morton Landon Award from the Academy of American Poets. The recipient of a Bess Hokin Prize from *Poetry*, a Pushcart Prize, and fellowships from the Ingram Merrill Foundation and the National Endowment for the Arts, his work has appeared in *The New Yorker*, *Boulevard*, *Poetry*, and elsewhere.

POETRY TITLES IN THE SERIES